Explore Telescopes

Lola Schaefer

Lerner Publications ◆ Minneapolis

Lerner Publications Company
An imprint of Lerner Publishing Group, Inc.
241 First Avenue North
Minneapolis, MN 55401 USA

For reading levels and more information, look up this title at www.lernerbooks.com.

Main body text set in Billy Infant Regular. Typeface provided by SparkType.

Library of Congress Cataloging-in-Publication Data

Names: Schaefer, Lola M., 1950- author.
Title: Explore telescopes / Lola Schaefer.
Description: Minneapolis: Lerner Publications, [2023] | Series: Lightning bolt books. Exploring space | Includes bibliographical references and index. | Audience: Ages 6-9 | Audience: Grades 2-3 | Summary: "Scientists use telescopes to see galaxies too far away to see in the night sky. But how do telescopes see so far? Readers learn how telescopes work and why scientists even send them into space"—Provided by publisher.
Identifiers: LCCN 2021045415 (print) | LCCN 2021045416 (ebook) | ISBN 9781728457833 (library binding) | ISBN 9781728463506 (paperback) | ISBN 9781728461618 (ebook)
Subjects: LCSH: Telescopes—Juvenile literature.
Classification: LCC QB88 .S33 2023 (print) | LCC QB88 (ebook) | DDC 522/.2—dc23/
   eng/20211108

LC record available at https://lccn.loc.gov/2021045415
LC ebook record available at https://lccn.loc.gov/2021045416

Manufactured in the United States of America
1-50811-50150-3/22/2022

Table of Contents

Pictures From Deep Space

Stars glow in deep space. Their light travels a long way and hits a mirror in a space telescope. A computer senses that light and measures it.

Planetariums often display images from space.

The computer sends the information to Earth. Scientists turn that information into pictures. They share those pictures with us so we can see light from galaxies far away.

The Story of Telescopes

In the 1600s, people made telescopes with curved glass lenses. These made objects on Earth look bigger than they usually look.

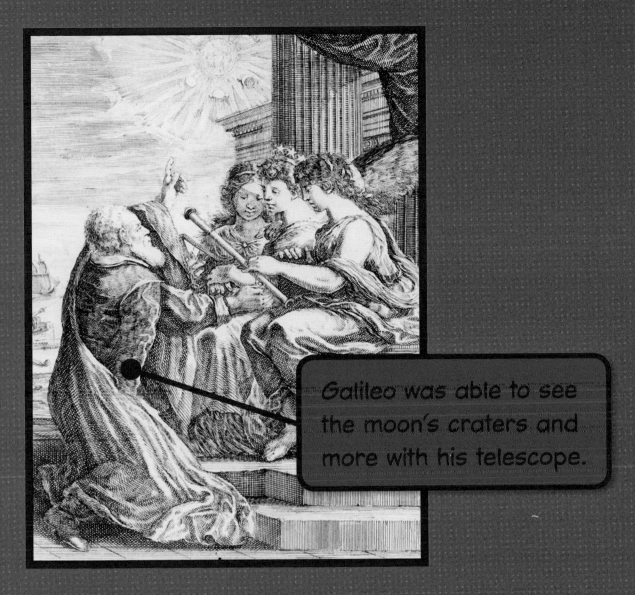

Galileo was able to see the moon's craters and more with his telescope.

Galileo Galilei was a scientist. He used telescopes to find objects in the sky. His telescope made objects look up to thirty times larger.

Refracting telescopes use lenses. They bend light. Faraway objects look much closer than they are.

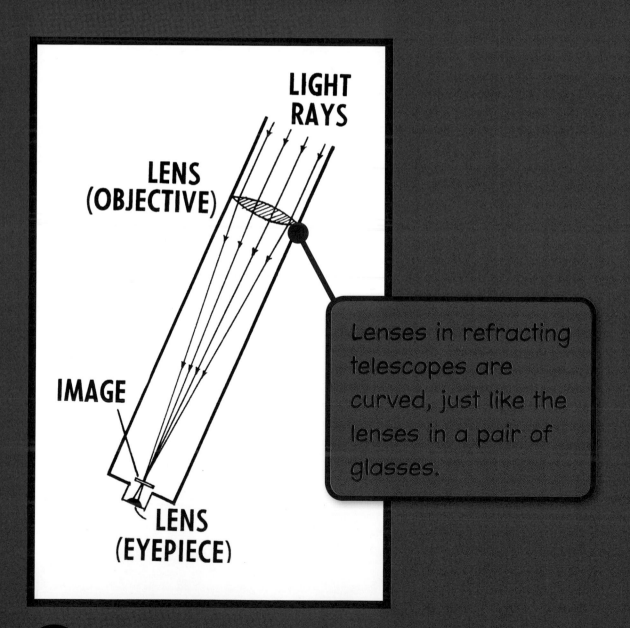

Lenses in refracting telescopes are curved, just like the lenses in a pair of glasses.

Many refracting telescopes can show planets and moons in our solar system.

Lenses need to be very thick and heavy to see far away. Those lenses are too heavy to send into space.

Reflecting telescopes use mirrors. They reflect light by bouncing it from one mirror to another. The first reflection is upside down. The second reflection is right side up.

Isaac Newton is often credited with building the first reflecting telescope.

The Hubble Space Telescope uses a mirror that is 8 feet (2.4 m) across.

Mirrors weigh less than lenses. Reflecting telescopes with mirrors can be sent into space. These telescopes are not heavy, but they are big and strong.

Telescopes in Action

Rockets launch telescopes into space. Space telescopes orbit Earth or the sun. They take pictures of different parts of space as they circle Earth and the sun.

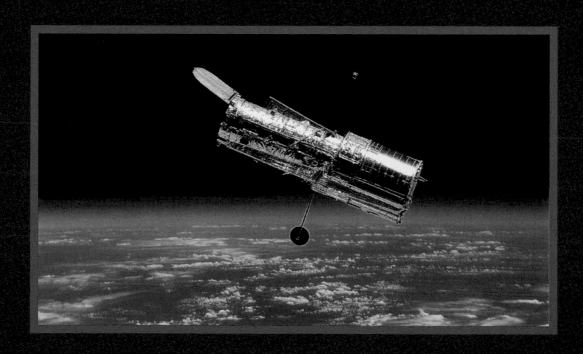

Winglike solar panels collect sunrays and make solar power. The solar panels also charge batteries. The batteries give power to the the rest of the telescope when the sun is covered.

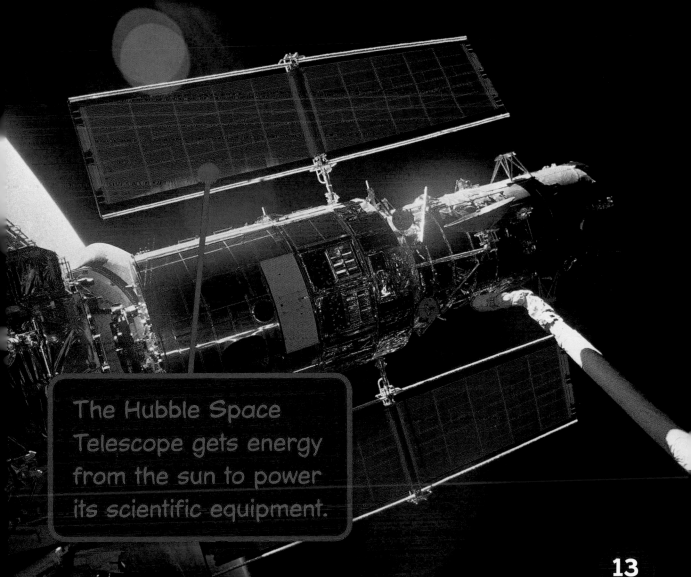

The Hubble Space Telescope gets energy from the sun to power its scientific equipment.

Light in space reflects off a large mirror. The image is upside down, so it hits a small mirror to flip it right side up. A computer then sends pictures of the light back to Earth.

Antennas on Earth receive information from space telescopes, and the information is sent to scientists to study.

The Hubble Space Telescope sends pictures of planets, stars, and galaxies. The Kepler Space Telescope can see planets orbiting stars outside our solar system.

Photos of faraway galaxies tell us a lot about what those galaxies are made of and how old they are.

Into the Unknown

The James Webb Space Telescope has larger mirrors than any other telescope. It orbits the sun far from Earth.

The James Webb Space Telescope needs to be very cold to work. A sunshield protects it from the sun's heat.

Hubble Ultra Deep Field
HST WFC3 IR

The Ultra Deep Field is the farthest point in space that we've been able to see, but the James Webb Space Telescope will see farther!

60″

F160W *H*
F125W *J*
F105W *Y*

N
E

The James Webb Space Telescope can see farther into space than other telescopes. In the future, it will send pictures of faraway places scientists have never seen before.

One day, you might make a bigger and better space telescope. And who knows what that telescope might find!

Telescope Diagram

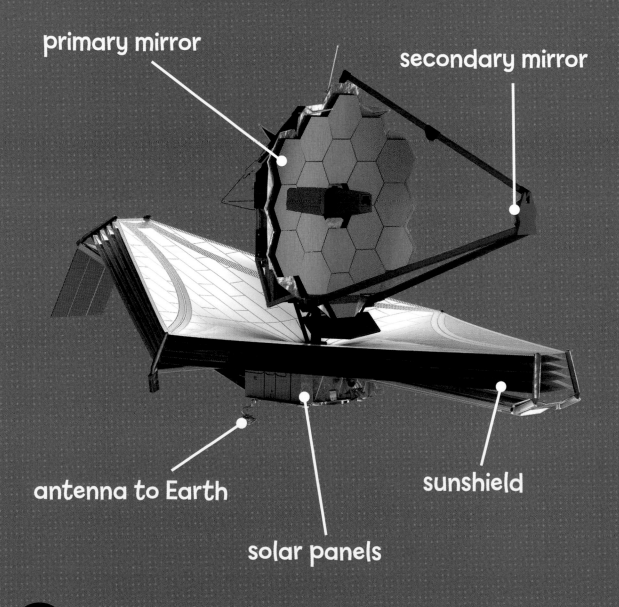

primary mirror

secondary mirror

antenna to Earth

solar panels

sunshield

From the Other Side of the Universe

Some space telescopes take pictures of light that we can see with our eyes. But we can't see some light, like infrared light. The James Webb Space Telescope can see infrared light and show us what it looks like. With this telescope, we can watch stars form and see galaxies no one has seen before.

Glossary

battery: a container filled with chemicals to produce electrical power

galaxy: one of the very large groups of stars, gas, and dust that make up the universe

lens: a clear curved piece of material used to bend the rays of light to form an image

mirror: a metal or glass surface that reflects images

orbit: the invisible path followed by an object circling another object

reflect: to bend or throw back

refract: when a light ray or sound wave changes speed or direction as it travels from one medium into another

sunshield: something put over a surface to protect it from heat and light

Learn More

Gater, Will. *The Mysteries of the Universe*. New York: DK, 2020.

Hamilton, John. *Hubble Space Telescope: Photographing the Universe*. Minneapolis: A&D Xtreme, 2018.

Kiddle: James Webb Space Telescope
https://kids.kiddle.co/James_Webb_Space _Telescope

Kids Discover: All about the Kepler Telescope, Our Wounded Space Scout
https://kidsdiscover.com/quick-reads/Kepler -telescope-wounded-space-scout/

NASA: Hubble Space Telescope
https://www.nasa.gov/mission_pages/hubble /main/index.html

Schaefer, Lola. *Explore Space Probes*. Minneapolis: Lerner Publications, 2023.

Index

Photo Acknowledgments

Image credits: NASA/ESA/V. Ksoll and D. Gouliermis (Universität Heidelberg), et al., p. 4; NataliyaBack/Shutterstock.com, p. 5; duncan1890/Getty Images, p. 6; Library of Congress/ LC-USZ62-110447, p. 7; Pearson Scott Foresman/Wikimedia Commons, p. 8; njnightsky/Getty Images, p. 9; belinski/Getty Images, p. 10; NASA, pp. 11, 13; Stocktrek/Getty Images, p. 12; NASA/Goddard/Rebecca Roth, p. 14; NASA/ESA/Hubble/L. Ho, J. Lee, and the PHANGS-HST Team, p. 15; NASA/Chris Gunn, p. 16; NASA/GSFC, p. 17; NASA/ESA/G. Illingworth (UCO/Lick Observatory and the University of California, Santa Cruz), R. Bouwens (UCO/Lick Observatory and Leiden University), HUDF09 Team, p. 18; Maica/Getty Images, p. 19; alex-mit/Getty Images, p. 20.

Cover: jamesbenet/Getty Images.